PUFFI

WHAT A GIGGLE!
More Kids' Jokes from Puffin

Before school jokes! After school jokes! Playground jokes! Jokes to tell instead of doing homework! *What a Giggle!* is bursting with snorts and giggles and hoots of laughter. Hundreds of jokes collected from kids like you all across Australia (including secret, naughty ones you should keep away from Mum and Dad).

Also by
Phillip Adams and Patrice Newell

What a Joke!
What a Laugh!

What a giggle!

More Kids' Jokes from Puffin

Collected by
Phillip Adams and Patrice Newell

Illustrated by
Terry Denton

PUFFIN BOOKS

Puffin Books
Penguin Books Australia Ltd
487 Maroondah Highway, PO Box 257
Ringwood, Victoria, 3134, Australia
Penguin Books Ltd
Harmondsworth, Middlesex, England
Penguin Putnam Inc.
375 Hudson Street, New York, New York 10014, USA
Penguin Books Canada Limited
10 Alcorn Avenue, Toronto, Ontario, Canada, M4V 3B2
Penguin Books (N.Z.) Ltd
Cnr Rosedale and Airborne Roads, Albany, Auckland, New Zealand
Penguin Books (South Africa) (Pty) Ltd
24 Sturdee Avenue, Rosebank, Johannesburg 2196, South Africa
Penguin Books India (P) Ltd
11, Community Centre, Panchsheel Park, New Delhi 110 017, India

First published by Penguin Books Australia, 1999

5 7 9 10 8 6

This selection Copyright © Phillip Adams and Patrice Newell, 1999
Illustrations Copyright © Terry Denton, 1999

The moral right of the authors and illustrator has been asserted

All rights reserved. Without limiting the rights under copyright
reserved above, no part of this publication may be reproduced,
stored in or introduced into a retrieval system, or transmitted,
in any form or by any means (electronic, mechanical, photocopying,
recording or otherwise), without the prior written permission
of both the copyright owner and the above publisher of this book.

Cover designed by Lynn Twelftree
Text designed by Beth McKinlay
Typeset in Gill Sans and Sassoon by Midland Typesetters,
Maryborough, Victoria
Printed and bound in Australia by McPherson's Printing Group, Maryborough, Victoria

National Library of Australia
Cataloguing-in-Publication data:

What a giggle! : more kids' jokes from puffin.

ISBN 0 14 1305010

1. Australian wit and humor - Juvenile literature.
2. Wit and humor, Juvenile. 3. Puns and punning - Juvenile literature. 4. Riddles, Juvenile.
I. Adams, Phillip, 1939- . II. Newell, Patrice, 1956- . III. Denton, Terry, 1950- .

808.882

This selection of jokes and riddles was first published in *The Penguin Book of Schoolyard Jokes*, collected by
Phillip Adams and Patrice Newell, published by Penguin Books Australia, 1997.

www.puffin.com.au

CONTENTS

Bags of Gags	1
Very Sick Jokes	15
Hot Dogs and Cool Cats	21
Fun and Games	31
Tucker Time	39
Howls, Yowls and Growls	63
Home Sweet Home	71
. . . Who's There?	81
Freaky but Funny	91
Animal Crackers	105
Crazy Classroom Capers	113
Funny Farm	121
Dumb and Dumber	131

Acknowledgements

Hundreds of children across Australia contributed to this collection, and special thanks go to our young technical advisers, Vidas Kubilius, Vaiva Kubilius and Rory Adams.

Teachers everywhere supported the idea for the book and asked students to write down their favourite jokes. Many thanks to Ian Burr, Michael Wright, Cathryn Ingle, Ross Deery, Heather Carter, Mark Evans and Melinda Archer. And Jean Menlove, Maria Clark and Ann Kubilius.

But the people to whom we're most indebted are the school children who found time to tell us what makes them laugh, especially those kids at Scone Public School, St Mary's, Scone, St James, Muswellbrook, Mullumbimby Adventist Primary School and Colonel Light Gardens Primary School.

bags of gags

What did the mosquito say the first time it saw the camel's hump?

'Did I do that?'

How do you make a hankie dance?

Put a little boogie in it.

WHAT A GIGGLE!

Where do you find the biggest spider?
> In the World Wide Web.

Did you hear about the man who didn't clean his glasses?
> He gave people dirty looks.

What do you call two robbers?

> A pair of nickers.

How can you talk to a fish?

> Drop it a line.

What's a bear's second favourite drink?

> Coca koala.

Why did the crab go to jail?

> Because it was always pinching things.

WHAT A GIGGLE!

What goes up when you count down?

                                        A rocket.

How many skunks does it take to stink out a room?

                                        A phew.

What is rude and only comes at Christmas?

                                        Rude-off.

Why do bees buzz?

                          Because they can't whistle.

BAGS OF GAGS

What did one eye say to the other?
'Something's come between us that smells.'

What sort of fish go meow?
Catfish.

WHAT A GIGGLE!

What do you find up a clean nose?

                              Fingerprints.

How do goldfish go into business?

                     They start on a small scale.

Why did the turtle cross the road?

                     To get to the shell station.

There were three tall men standing under the umbrella and none of them got wet. How could that be?

> It wasn't raining.

What do you call a person who can sing and drink lemonade at the same time?

> A pop singer.

Where do tadpoles change into frogs?

> In the croakroom.

Can a shoe box?

> No, but a tin can.

WHAT A GIGGLE!

Why do snakes have forked tongues?
> Because they can't use chopsticks.

What has a hundred legs but can't walk?
> Fifty pairs of pants.

What would you call Superman if he lost all his powers?
> Man.

Why are Saturday and Sunday so strong?
> Because the rest are week days.

Where does a whale sleep?

> On the sea bed.

Why is it easy to weigh fish?
> Because they come with scales.

WHAT A GIGGLE!

Tarzan flying through the air,
Tarzan lost his underwear,
Tarzan said, 'me no care,
Jane make me another pair.'

Why did the light turn red?
　　　Wouldn't you turn red if you were caught
　　　　　changing in the middle of the street?

What animals on Noah's ark didn't come in pairs?
> Worms. They came in apples.

What did one ear say to the other?
> 'Between you and me we have brains.'

One One was a racehorse
Two Two was one too
One One won one race
Two Two won one too.

What starts with 'T' ends with 'T' and is full of 'T'?
> A teapot.

WHAT A GIGGLE!

W hat goes up in the air white and comes down yellow and white?

An egg.

W here does Thursday come before Wednesday?

In the dictionary.

What kind of shoes does a toad wear?
> Open toad sandals.

What goes up on your birthday but never comes down?
> Your age.

What do astronauts make their pyjamas out of?
> Saturn.

What happens when a frog's car breaks down?
> It gets toad away.

Very sick jokes

What's green, red, disgusting and makes a gluggy noise?

                      A frog in the blender.

How do you take a sick pig to hospital?

                      In a ham-bulance.

What's faster, heat or cold?

                      Heat, you can catch a cold.

'Doctor, tell me, can a child of twelve take out his appendix?'
'Certainly not Madam.'
'Did you hear that, Johnny? Now put them back!'

What do ants take when they are sick?
                              Antibiotics.

When do people with the flu get exercise?
                              When their noses run.

What is the best thing to take into the desert?
                              A thirst aid kit.

What goes through a grasshopper's mind when it hits the windscreen of a car going at 100 kilometres per hour?

Its legs.

What did the first tonsil say to the second tonsil?
'Better get dressed up tonight, we're going out.'

WHAT A GIGGLE!

'Doctor, doctor, I keep thinking I'm a fruitcake!'
'What's got into you?'
'Flour, raisins, sultanas and cherries!'

'Doctor, doctor, you've got to help me, I think I'm a bridge!'
'What's come over you?'
'So far two cars, a truck and a motorbike.'

'I think you need glasses.'
'But I already wear glasses.'
'In that case I need some too.'

VERY SICK JOKES

'Doctor, doctor, my hair keeps falling out, can you give me something to keep it in?'
      'Sure, what about this clean jar?'

'Doctor, doctor, I keep hearing ringing in my ears.'
      'Well, where did you expect to hear it?'

hot dogs and cool cats

There are three dogs and three men, and they have to get across the desert without the dogs making a mess. The first man gets a quarter of the way across when, unfortunately, his dog does a poo. The second man gets halfway when his dog also does a poo. But the last man gets all the way. How did he do it?
'Me not silly, me not dumb, me stick cork up doggy's bum.'

WHAT A GIGGLE!

How do you spell 'mouse trap' using three letters?

C A T.

What did the dog say when he sat on sandpaper?
'Rough! Rough!'

'Ouch, I thought you said your dog didn't bite?'
'That's not my dog.'

What kind of cat helps you fix things?
A tool kit.

Why did the man bring his dog to the railway station?
To train him.

What kind of cat is found in a library?
A catalogue.

WHAT A GIGGLE!

I'd like to have your picture
It would look very nice.
I'd put it in the cellar
And frighten all the mice.

What's a dog's favourite fruit?
                                                              Paw paw.

Now you see it, now you don't, now you see it, now you don't. What is it?
                A black cat on a zebra crossing.

How can you stop your dog barking in the hall?
                      Put him in the backyard.

HOT DOGS AND COOL CATS

If ten cats were on a boat and one jumped out, how many would be left?

>None, they were all copycats.

Why did the kitten join the Red Cross?

>Because it wanted to be a first aid kit.

What dog never barks?

>A hot dog.

What is every cat's favourite nursery rhyme?
>'Three Blind Mice'.

What has a coat all winter and pants in summer?
> A dog.

If a cat fell into a rubbish bin what would you call it?
> Kitty litter.

What's the difference between a well-dressed man and a dog?
> The man wears a suit and the dog just pants.

What happened to the cat who ate a ball of wool?

>She had mittens.

One flea says to the other as he walks down the road: 'Shall we keep on walking or catch a dog?'

WHAT A GIGGLE!

Why did the Dalmation go to the cleaners?

> His coat had spots all over it.

If you crossed a dog with a fax machine, what would you get?

> A fax terrier.

HOT DOGS AND COOL CATS

Why do cats change their size?
Because they are let out at night and taken in in the morning.

Why did the dog tick?
Because it was a watch dog.

What do you call a three-legged dog?
Skippy.

What's more fantastic than a talking dog?
A spelling bee.

freaky but funny

Two bats were out one night looking for blood, but after a few hours of unsuccessful hunting they decided to go home. In the wee hours of the morning, one of the bats was so hungry he said he had to go out hunting again. An hour later he came back all covered in blood.
'Where did you get that blood?' said the other bat, full of envy.
'Come with me and I'll show you.' So out they went into the night.
'See that tree over there?' said the bat covered in blood.
'Yeah.'
'Well, I didn't!'

WHAT A GIGGLE!

W hat's a skeleton afraid of?

        A dog. Because it likes bones.

W hat trees do ghosts like?

        Ceme-trees.

What happened when Frankenstein met a girl monster?

> They fell in love at first fright.

Why are vampires stupid?

> Because they're suckers.

Where would you find a one-handed monster?

> In a second hand store.

What do space aliens eat for breakfast?

> Flying sausages.

WHAT A GIGGLE!

W hat does a monster eat after he's been to the dentist?

> The dentist.

H ow do we know the letter 'S' is scary?
> Because it makes cream, scream.

'Hey, brother ghost, how did you get that terrible bump on your head?'

'I was floating through the key hole when some moron put the key back in the lock.'

How many vampires does it take to change a light globe?

None, they prefer the dark.

What happened to the wolf that fell into the washing machine?

It became a wash and werewolf.

Why does a witch ride a broom?

Because vacuum cleaners are too heavy.

What do ghosts do every night at one a.m.?

> Take a coffin break.

What's a monster's favourite sport?

> Squash.

'I've just bought a haunted bike.'
'How do you know it's haunted?'
'Because it's got spooks on the wheels.'

What kind of spook can you hold on the end of your finger?

> A bogey.

FREAKY BUT FUNNY

Why didn't the vampire want to play cricket?
Because he didn't want to damage his bats.

Did you hear about the skeleton that was attacked by a dog?
It ran off with some bones and left him without a leg to stand on.

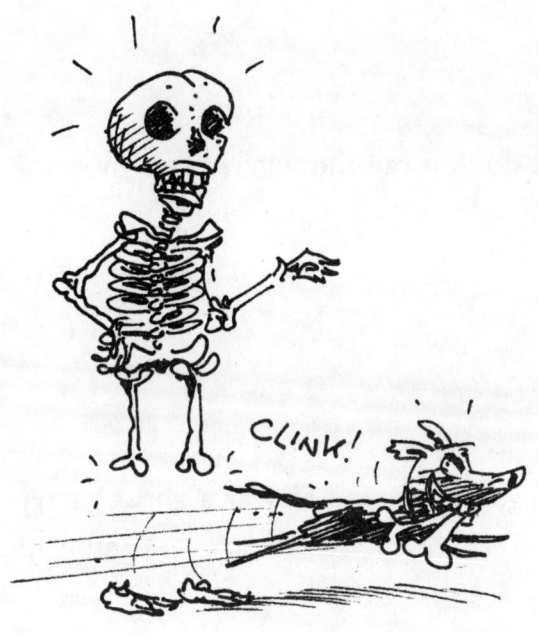

WHAT A GIGGLE!

What do you call the winner of a monster beauty contest?

　　　　　　　　　　　　　　　　Ugly.

What games do you play at a ghost party?
　　　　　　　　　　　　Haunt and seek.

FREAKY BUT FUNNY

What's a ghost's favourite bird?

> A scarecrow.

How do you make a skeleton laugh?

> Tickle its funny bone.

What do witches put on their hair?

> Scare spray.

Did you hear about the ghost that ate all the Christmas decorations?

> He got tinsellitis.

WHAT A GIGGLE!

Why didn't the skeleton go to the dance?
> He had no body to go with.

What do little ghosts play with?
> Deady bears.

What did the mother ghost say to the baby ghost?
> 'Don't spook until you're spoken to.'

Why are vampires like stars?
> Because they only come out at night.

What song do ghosts hate the most?
> 'Staying alive, staying alive, ha ha ha ha staying alive.'

What do you do with a green monster?
> Put it in the sun until it ripens.

WHAT A GIGGLE!

What did the ghost buy his wife for her birthday?
> A see-through nightie.

What's every monster's favourite part of the newspaper?
> The horror-scope.

Why don't ghosts make good magicians?
> You can see right through their tricks.

What is a waste of energy?
> Telling hair-raising stories to a bald man.

FREAKY BUT FUNNY

What do you call a dumb skeleton?

A numbskull.

Which street does a ghost live in?

A dead end street.

animal crackers

A bear and a rabbit are doing a poo in the forest, when the bear turns to the rabbit and enquires: 'Does your poo ever stick to your fur?'
'No.'
So the bear wiped his bum with the rabbit.

WHAT A GIGGLE!

What happened to the elephant who drank too much beer?

> He got trunk.

Why don't snakes have a sense of humour?
> Because you can't pull their legs.

ANIMAL CRACKERS

What do you call a mouse if you put it in the freezer?

Mice.

How can you find an elephant in your bed?
Because it'll have a big 'E' on its pyjamas.

What do you get if you cross a skunk with a bear?

Winnie the Pooh.

What does a frog drink when he's on a diet?
Diet croak.

WHAT A GIGGLE!

What bird is a good cook?

                                        A kookaburra.

What's the difference between an elephant and a flea?
  An elephant can have fleas, but a flea can't have elephants.

Where do frogs keep their money?

                                        In the riverbank.

'**I** want that bird!'
'It's all yours, madam, but it costs twenty dollars.'
'Will you send me the bill?'
'No, you have to take the whole bird.'

ANIMAL CRACKERS

W hy did the elephant go backwards into the telephone box?

> He wanted to reverse the charges.

W hat do you call an owl with a sore throat?

> A bird that doesn't give a hoot.

WHAT A GIGGLE!

What is a slug?
> A snail with a housing problem.

How do you make an elephant fly?
> Push him off the top of a highrise building.

ANIMAL CRACKERS

What's a frog's favourite drink?

　　　　　　　　　　　Croaka cola.

Why is the sky so high?
　　　So birds won't bump their heads.

What sort of lollies do koalas eat?

　　　　　　　　　　　Chewing gum.

What do you call a hitchhiking elephant?
　　　　　A two-tonne pick up truck.

crazy classroom capers

'Miss, can I go to the toilet please?'
'Yes, Johnny, but I want you to say the alphabet first.'
'OK ... ABCDEFGHIJKLMNOQRSTUVWXYZ.'
'But where's the 'P'?'
'Running down my leg, Miss.'

WHAT A GIGGLE!

'Class, class! I wish you'd pay a little attention!'
'Well, we are,' said Sally, 'as little as possible.'

'Polly, did your mother help you with your homework last night?'

'No. She did it for me.'

What's a good way of stopping pollution in schools?

Use unleaded pencils.

'Why are you writing so slowly, Johnny?'
'Because it's a letter to my friend who can't read fast.'

How do you make a sausage roll?
> Push it down the hill.

Why did the strawberry need a lawyer?
> Because it was in a jam.

What's a cannibal's favourite game?
> Swallow the leader.

Why didn't the duck eat his soup?
> He couldn't find his quackers.

WHAT A GIGGLE!

Why did the orange stop rolling down the hill?
> Because it ran out of juice.

Where do vegetables take their rusty cars for a service?
> To the car-rot station.

What cup can't you drink from?
> A hiccup.

Why won't you ever be hungry at the beach?
> Because of all the sand-which-is there.

TUCKER TIME

How do you know when you have a hundred puppies trying to get into your fridge?

You can't shut the door.

What's the best thing to put into a pie?

Your teeth.

WHAT A GIGGLE!

Why did the girl throw the butter out the window?

> Because she wanted to see the butterfly.

What do you get when you cross a potato with an onion?

> A potato with watery eyes.

What did the cannibal have for breakfast?
>Baked Beings.

Why did the orange cross the road?
>Because he wanted to show his girlfriend how to play squash.

What vegetable has a heart in its head?
>A lettuce.

What type of bread is the best for an actor?
>A large roll.

WHAT A GIGGLE!

What did one egg say to another?

'You're cracked.'

What do thieves eat?

Takeaway.

What do traffic wardens have in their sandwiches?

Traffic jam.

What has a hole in the middle and no beginning or end?

A doughnut.

TUCKER TIME

What can a cook make with the letter 'Y'?

> A cooky.

What day do chickens hate the most?

> Fry days.

howls, yowls and growls

How do you get five elephants into a small car?
Two in the front, two in the back and one in the glove compartment.

How do you fit five rhinoceroses in a car?
Chuck the elephants out.

WHAT A GIGGLE!

W hat do you call a camel with no humps?

A horse.

W hat do you get when you cross a bear and a kangaroo?

A fur coat with big pockets.

HOWLS, YOWLS AND GROWLS

What type of underwear do zebras wear?

Z-bra.

When do elephants have sixteen feet?

When there are four of them.

What do you get if you cross a giraffe with a hedgehog?

A ten metre toothbrush.

What's a lion's favourite dance?

Lion-dancing.

WHAT A GIGGLE!

What can you do when a tiger eats your dictionary?

> *Take the words out of its mouth.*

If horses wear horse shoes, what do camels wear?

> *Desert boots.*

What do elephants play in the car?

> *Squash.*

Why don't kangaroos ride bikes?
Because they don't have a thumb to ring the bell.

HOWLS, YOWLS AND GROWLS

W hat do you do if an elephant sits in front of you at the movies?

>Miss most of the movie.

W hat has four legs, eight feet and three tails?
>An elephant with spare parts.

WHAT A GIGGLE!

What is big, red and has a trunk?

                A sunburnt elephant.

What's worse than a giraffe with a sore throat?

                A centipede with blisters.

HOWLS, YOWLS AND GROWLS

What do you get if you cross Santa with a tiger?
Santa Claws.

Who went into the lion's den and came out alive?

The lion.

Why do giraffes have such long necks?
Because their feet stink.

What's the same size and shape as an elephant but weights nothing?

An elephant's shadow.

home sweet home

'Mum, I'm tired of looking like everyone else, could you part my hair from ear to ear, please?
'Are you sure?'
'Yeah.'
That day Johnny came home from school really depressed.
'Can you do my hair back the other way again, Mum?'
'What's the matter, Johnny, are you sick of being different already?'
'It's not that. I can't stand people whispering in my nose.'

WHAT A GIGGLE!

'Sally, why have you put sugar in your pillow?'
　　　　'So I'll have sweet dreams, Mum.'

What has four legs and doesn't walk?
　　　　　　　　　　　A table.

'Mum, can I have a dollar for the man who's crying in the park?'
'What's he crying about?'
'He's crying, "Hot dogs, one dollar!"'

'Get your father out of that fridge!'
　　　　'But I want a cool pop, Mum.'

HOME SWEET HOME

'Why are you jumping up and down, Johnny?'
'I took my medicine, but I forgot to shake the bottle.'

What's grey, wrinkled and hangs out your underwear?

Your grandma.

WHAT A GIGGLE!

What's the easiest way to get on TV?

Sit on it.

'Sally, what are you doing home so early, I thought you had baseball practice?'

'I did, but I hit the ball over the fence and the coach told me to run home.'

'Dad, have you ever seen an oil well?'
'Why, no son, I haven't. But I haven't seen one sick either.'

Why are tall people cleaner than short people?
Because they're in the shower longer.

'Mum, are we poisonous snakes?'
'No, of course not.'
'Just as well, because I just bit my lip.'

What did the girl say to her grandfather when he was drowning?

'Paddle Pop!'

WHAT A GIGGLE!

'Johnny, how are you enjoying your new guitar?'

'I threw it away, Dad. It had a hole in the middle.'

What's brown, hairy and has no legs but walks?

Dad's socks.

'Sally, this salad tastes awful. Did you wash the lettuce like I asked you?'

'Yes, Mum, and I used soap too.'

'Dad, what did the X-ray of your brain show?'

'Uh, nothing much, son.'

HOME SWEET HOME

'Mum, why isn't my nose twelve inches long?'
    'Because then it would be a foot.'

'Daddy, can you see any change in me?'
'No, why son?'
'Because I just swallowed twenty cents.'

WHAT A GIGGLE!

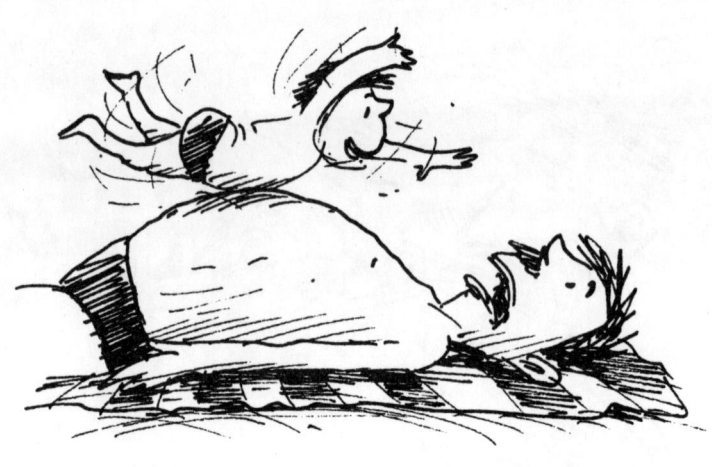

'Mum, can I swim on a full stomach?'
    'No, Johnny, it's better to swim on water.'

Why do little brothers chew with their mouths open?

        Flies have got to live somewhere.

HOME SWEET HOME

'Eat your cabbage up, Johnny, it will put colour in your cheeks!'

'But I don't want green cheeks, Mum.'

What has many rings but no fingers?

A telephone.

'Dad, I just can't work on an empty stomach!'

'Well, try the table then!'

'Why did you sleep with a ruler last night, Johnny?'

'Because I wanted to see how long I slept, Mum!'

... Who's there?

Knock knock.
Who's there?
Bear.
Bear who?
Bear bum.

WHAT A GIGGLE!

Knock knock.
Who's there?
Granny.
Granny who?
Knock knock.
Who's there?
Granny.
Granny who?
Knock knock.
Who's there?
Granny.
Granny who?
Knock knock.
Who's there?
Aunt.
Aunt who?
Aunt you glad Granny's gone!

Knock knock.
Who's there?
Oscar.
Oscar who?
Oscar silly question, get a silly answer.

Knock knock.
Who's there?
The Sultan.
The Sultan who?
The sultan pepper.

Knock knock.
Who's there?
Liz.
Liz who?
Lizen only once because I'm not going to repeat myself.

WHAT A GIGGLE!

Knock knock.
Who's there?
Lion.
Lion who?
Lying won't get you anywhere.

Knock knock.
Who's there?
Canoe.
Canoe who?
Canoe please get off my foot.

Knock knock.
Who's there?
Sancho.
Sancho who?
Sancho a letter, but you never answered.

Knock knock.
Who's there?
Dwayne.
Dwayne who?
Dwayne the bathtub, I'm drowning!

Knock knock.
Who's there?
Nick.
Nick who?
Nick off.

WHAT A GIGGLE!

Knock knock.
Who's there?
Celia.
Celia who?
Celia later alligator.

Knock knock.
Who's there?
Cows go.
Cows go who?
Cows don't go who, they go moo.

Knock knock.
Who's there?
Isabel.
Isabel who?
Isabel necessary on a bicycle?

Knock knock.
Who's there?
Herman.
Herman who?
Herman eggs.

Knock knock.
Who's there?
Snow.
Snow who?
Snow good asking me.

WHAT A GIGGLE!

Knock knock.
Who's there?
Satin.
Satin who?
Who satin my chair?

Knock knock.
Who's there?
Betty.
Betty who?
Betty late than never.

Knock knock.
Who's there?
Sue.
Sue who?
Sue-prise, it's me.

... WHO'S THERE?

Knock knock.
Who's there?
Barbie.
Barbie who?
Barbie Q.

Knock knock.
Who's there?
Carrie.
Carrie who?
Carrie me inside, I'm exhausted.

freaky but funny

Two bats were out one night looking for blood, but after a few hours of unsuccessful hunting they decided to go home. In the wee hours of the morning, one of the bats was so hungry he said he had to go out hunting again. An hour later he came back all covered in blood.
'Where did you get that blood?' said the other bat, full of envy.
'Come with me and I'll show you.' So out they went into the night.
'See that tree over there?' said the bat covered in blood.
'Yeah.'
'Well, I didn't!'

WHAT A GIGGLE!

What's a skeleton afraid of?

> A dog. Because it likes bones.

What trees do ghosts like?

> Ceme-trees.

What happened when Frankenstein met a girl monster?
> They fell in love at first fright.

Why are vampires stupid?
> Because they're suckers.

Where would you find a one-handed monster?
> In a second hand store.

What do space aliens eat for breakfast?
> Flying sausages.

WHAT A GIGGLE!

W hat does a monster eat after he's been to the dentist?

> The dentist.

H ow do we know the letter 'S' is scary?
> Because it makes cream, scream.

'Hey, brother ghost, how did you get that terrible bump on your head?'
'I was floating through the key hole when some moron put the key back in the lock.'

How many vampires does it take to change a light globe?

None, they prefer the dark.

What happened to the wolf that fell into the washing machine?

It became a wash and werewolf.

Why does a witch ride a broom?

Because vacuum cleaners are too heavy.

WHAT A GIGGLE!

What do ghosts do every night at one a.m.?
>Take a coffin break.

What's a monster's favourite sport?
>Squash.

'**I**'ve just bought a haunted bike.'
'How do you know it's haunted?'
'Because it's got spooks on the wheels.'

What kind of spook can you hold on the end of your finger?
>A bogey.

FREAKY BUT FUNNY

Why didn't the vampire want to play cricket?
>Because he didn't want to damage his bats.

Did you hear about the skeleton that was attacked by a dog?
>It ran off with some bones and left him without a leg to stand on.

WHAT A GIGGLE!

What do you call the winner of a monster beauty contest?

Ugly.

What games do you play at a ghost party?

Haunt and seek.

FREAKY BUT FUNNY

What's a ghost's favourite bird?

>A scarecrow.

How do you make a skeleton laugh?

>Tickle its funny bone.

What do witches put on their hair?

>Scare spray.

Did you hear about the ghost that ate all the Christmas decorations?

>He got tinsellitis.

WHAT A GIGGLE!

Why didn't the skeleton go to the dance?
> He had no body to go with.

What do little ghosts play with?
> Deady bears.

What did the mother ghost say to the baby ghost?
> 'Don't spook until you're spoken to.'

Why are vampires like stars?
> Because they only come out at night.

What song do ghosts hate the most?
> 'Staying alive, staying alive, ha ha ha ha staying alive.'

What do you do with a green monster?
> Put it in the sun until it ripens.

WHAT A GIGGLE!

What did the ghost buy his wife for her birthday?
A see-through nightie.

What's every monster's favourite part of the newspaper?
The horror-scope.

Why don't ghosts make good magicians?
You can see right through their tricks.

What is a waste of energy?
Telling hair-raising stories to a bald man.

FREAKY BUT FUNNY

What do you call a dumb skeleton?

A numbskull.

Which street does a ghost live in?

A dead end street.

aNimal crackers

A bear and a rabbit are doing a poo in the forest, when the bear turns to the rabbit and enquires: 'Does your poo ever stick to your fur?'
'No.'
So the bear wiped his bum with the rabbit.

WHAT A GIGGLE!

What happened to the elephant who drank too much beer?

> He got trunk.

Why don't snakes have a sense of humour?
> Because you can't pull their legs.

What do you call a mouse if you put it in the freezer?

>   Mice.

How can you find an elephant in your bed?
> Because it'll have a big 'E' on its pyjamas.

What do you get if you cross a skunk with a bear?

> Winnie the Pooh.

What does a frog drink when he's on a diet?
> Diet croak.

WHAT A GIGGLE!

What bird is a good cook?

A kookaburra.

What's the difference between an elephant and a flea?

An elephant can have fleas, but a flea can't have elephants.

Where do frogs keep their money?

In the riverbank.

'**I** want that bird!'
'It's all yours, madam, but it costs twenty dollars.'
'Will you send me the bill?'
'No, you have to take the whole bird.'

ANIMAL CRACKERS

Why did the elephant go backwards into the telephone box?

> He wanted to reverse the charges.

What do you call an owl with a sore throat?

> A bird that doesn't give a hoot.

WHAT A GIGGLE!

What is a slug?
> A snail with a housing problem.

How do you make an elephant fly?
> Push him off the top of a highrise building.

ANIMAL CRACKERS

What's a frog's favourite drink?

>Croaka cola.

Why is the sky so high?

>So birds won't bump their heads.

What sort of lollies do koalas eat?

>Chewing gum.

What do you call a hitchhiking elephant?

>A two-tonne pick up truck.

crazy classroom capers

'Miss, can I go to the toilet please?'
'Yes, Johnny, but I want you to say the alphabet first.'
'OK ... ABCDEFGHIJKLMNOQRSTUVWXYZ.'
'But where's the 'P'?'
'Running down my leg, Miss.'

WHAT A GIGGLE!

'Class, class! I wish you'd pay a little attention!'
'Well, we are,' said Sally, 'as little as possible.'

'Polly, did your mother help you with your homework last night?'

'No. She did it for me.'

What's a good way of stopping pollution in schools?

Use unleaded pencils.

'Why are you writing so slowly, Johnny?'
'Because it's a letter to my friend who can't read fast.'

CRAZY CLASSROOM CAPERS

Why did the boy take a car to school?
>Because he wanted to drive his teacher up the wall.

What do you call a biscuit that's good at school?
>A smart cookie.

WHAT A GIGGLE!

'We're going to study the English kings and queens today. Now, who can tell me who came after Mary?'

'One of her little lambs?'

Why was the science teacher's head wet?
Because she had a brainstorm.

'Now, class, there will only be half a day of school this morning.'
'Hooray!'
'The other half will be this afternoon.'

When is a green book not a green book?
>   When it's read.

What starts with an 'E' and ends with an 'E' but only has one letter in it?
>   An envelope.

Why didn't anyone take the bus to school?
>   Because it wouldn't fit through the door.

Why did the boy bring a ladder to school?
>Because he wanted to go to high school.

'**N**ow that you've sat for your exams, Johnny, how did you find the questions?'
>'The questions were easy, I found the answers hard.'

Why did the thermometer go to college?
>Because it wanted to get a degree.

'**S**usie, it gives me great pleasure to give you 89 out of 100 for your science project.'
>'Why not give me 100 out of 100 and really enjoy yourself?'

CRAZY CLASSROOM CAPERS

'Now, if you asked your mother for a dollar and then you asked your father for a dollar, how much would you have?'
'One dollar.'
'Can't you add up?'
'Well, Miss, you don't know my dad.'

What do music teachers give you?

Sound advice.

funny farm

When does a mouse need an umbrella?
>When it's raining cats and dogs.

'Did you know it takes three sheep to make a jumper?'
>'I didn't even know they could knit.'

WHAT A GIGGLE!

Why is it hard to have a conversation with a goat around?

>Because it always butts in.

What does a farmer give his wife on St Valentine's day?

>Hogs and kisses.

FUNNY FARM

Why did the farmer buy a brown cow?
> Because he wanted chocolate milk.

What do pigs do after school?
> Their hamwork.

What's grey with a blue face?
> A mouse holding its breath.

What TV show is about investigating mysterious cattle?
> 'The Ox-Files'.

WHAT A GIGGLE!

In what book do ducks look up words?

                                        A duck-tionary.

What kind of cow can you sit on?

                                        A cow-ch.

What do pigs wear to bed?

                                        Pig-jamas.

What do you get if you cross a rabbit and a sheep?

                                        A jumper.

FUNNY FARM

What do you call a pig in a restaurant?

                        A pig out.

What do you call a cow that eats your grass?

                        A lawn mooer.

WHAT A GIGGLE!

Why do cows wear bells?
>Because their horns don't work.

What mouse won't eat cheese?
>A computer mouse.

Why did the chicken cross the playground?
>To get to the other slide.

What do you call a cow with no legs?
>Ground beef.

FUNNY FARM

How did the farmer mend his pants?
>With cabbage patches.

Which singer do cows prefer?
>Moodonna.

WHAT A GIGGLE!

W hat do cows drink?

Cowpuccino.

W hat's the easiest way to count cows?

On a cow-culator.

FUNNY FARM

What do you call high-rise flats for pigs?

　　　　　　　　　　　　Sty scrapers.

What did the apple tree say to the farmer?

　　　　　　　　　　　　Stop picking on me.

What game do hogs play?

　　　　　　　　　　　　Pig pong.

What do you get when you cross a karate expert with a pig?

　　　　　　　　　　　　A pork chop.

dumb and dumber

The Queen was showing the Archbishop around her stables, when one of her prize thoroughbreds let off a huge, loud fart.
'Oh, I am sorry,' said the Queen. 'How embarrassing.'
'It's perfectly all right, Your Majesty, as a matter of fact, I thought it was the horse.'

WHAT A GIGGLE!

What walks through the forest with sixteen legs?
Snow White and the Seven Dwarves.

What goes up and wobbles?

A jelly-copter.

DUMB AND DUMBER

What goes zzub zzub zzub?

A bee flying backwards.

There are four people named Everybody, Somebody, Anybody and Nobody.
There was an important job to be done and Everybody was asked to do it.
Everybody was sure Somebody would do it.
Anybody could have done it, but Nobody did it.
Somebody got angry about that, because it was Everybody's job.
Everybody thought Anybody could do it, but Nobody realised that Everybody wouldn't do it.
It ended up that Everybody blamed Somebody for what Anybody could have done.

What horse never wears a saddle?

A seahorse.

WHAT A GIGGLE!

What do you call a woman in the distance?

                                          Dot.

What do you call a man in a pile of leaves?

                                   Russell.

What do you call a boy with a rabbit cage on his head?

                                   Warren.

What do you call a girl with a frog on her head?

                                       Lily.

What do you call a man with no arms and no legs floating out at sea?

Bob.

What do you call a man with a spade on his head?

Doug.

What do you call a man with a car on his head?

Jack.

Where can you find the most cows?

Moo York.

WHAT A GIGGLE!

Why was Mummy centipede so upset?
> All the kids needed new shoes.

What has wheels and flies?
> A garbage truck.

DUMB AND DUMBER

'Did you hear about the wooden car?'
'No.'
'It wooden go.'

What makes suits and eats spinach?
                        Popeye the Tailorman.

Why did the dinosaur cross the road?
    Because the chicken hadn't been invented yet.

There was an old woman from Leeds,
Who swallowed a packet of seeds.
In less than an hour,
Her nose grew a flower,
And her hair was all covered in weeds.

What do you call a chocolate easter bunny that has stayed in the sun too long?

> A runny bunny.

Which rock singer has a vegie garden on her head?

> Tina Turnip.

Where does Tarzan get his clothes from?
> The jungle sale.

If you were locked in a room with only a calendar and a bed, how could you survive?
> You could eat the dates from the calendar and drink from the springs in the bed.

DUMB AND DUMBER

What goes ha ha ha ha THUMP!
> A person laughing their head off.

Fatty and Skinny went to Mars,
Fatty came back with lots of bras.

WHAT A GIGGLE!

What do you do if your toe drops off in the middle of the road?

> Call a toe truck.

Why do bees have sticky hair?
> Because they use honey combs.

What do you get when you stack toads together?
>A toadempole.

How do you make a bandstand?
>Hide all the chairs.

What nuts can be found in space?
>Astronuts.

If you invited all the alphabet to tea who would be late?
>The letters 'UVWXYZ' because they all come after 'T'.

WHAT A GIGGLE!

What is a ten letter word that starts with gas?
>Automobile.

'Dinosaur?'
'No.'
'Do you think he saurus?'

Why are hairdressers never late for work?
>Because they take short cuts.

'Sally, have you given the goldfish fresh water today?'
>'No, they haven't finished the water they had yesterday.'

DUMB AND DUMBER

Why do fish have such huge phone bills?
> Because when they get on the line, they can't get off.

What does the sun drink out of?
> Sunglasses.

WHAT A GIGGLE!

Fatty and Skinny climbed a tree,
Fatty fell down the lavatory.
Skinny went down to pull the chain,
And Fatty was never seen again.

What planet has the biggest bottom?

> Sat on.

DUMB AND DUMBER

Why is an old car like a baby?
> It never goes anywhere without a rattle.

How many animals can you put in an empty cage?
> One. After that it's not empty.

What is the tallest building in any city?
> The library, because it has the most storeys.

What do you call a boomerang that won't come back?
> A stick.

WHAT A GIGGLE!

What do frogs sit on?

>Toadstools.

What happened to the pot plant on the window-sill in the maths class?

>It grew square roots.

DUMB AND DUMBER

What is green and plays the guitar.

> Elvis Parsley.

Why does a dog sit on its hind legs?

> If it didn't it would be standing up.

Why couldn't the bicycle stand up?

> Because it was tyred.

What's black and white and red all over?

> A newspaper.

WHAT A GIGGLE!

What is the egg capital of the world?

　　　　　　　　　　　　New Yolk City.

What do you call a rich fish?

　　　　　　　　　　　　A goldfish.

Why do bees itch?

　　　　　　　　　　　　Because they have hives.

What lies in a pram and wobbles?

　　　　　　　　　　　　A jelly baby.

DUMB AND DUMBER

W hat do you get from a nervous cow?

A milk shake.

W hat do you call an egg that knows everything?

An eggs-pert.

WHAT A GIGGLE!

What type of pants do scientists wear?

Genes.

What do you call a smelly Father Christmas?

Farter Claus.